Acknowledgements

GDM would like to thank:

his family

bride, Norma
daughters, Laura and Anna
parents, Marty and Weezie
John, Carrie, Robert (brother, sister, brother)

lovers of poetry

Ron and Mark

creative sparks

Norman Goldblatt
Robert Ginsberg
Mark Eleveld
Marc Smith
Daisaku Ikeda

loyal friends

Michelle Mega
Christy Sherbrook
Tony Weatherington

EM Press, LLC
709 Marion St. Joliet, IL 60436
www.em-press.com

Knowles Printing

Cover Design/image manipulation
Gregory Harms/FARMHOUSE/ga
www.farmhouse-ga.com

ISBN 0-9708012-1-1

07/18/02

Kathy,

Let us be bearers of light as we transform our society...

Children of Kosen-Rufu

George David Miller

:: Problematic Parables

:: Elegies on Education

:: Suburban Soliloquies

:: Tender Tirades

:: Children of Kosen-Rufu

:: Metaphysical Mischief

:: Funereal Fragments

Problematic Parables

bearers of light
like you, me, and Prometheus
are deemed arsonists
by fire departments
devoted to extinguishing truth

these fire departments
would rather us raze
their villages to cinders
than enlighten just one soul

because they see
that our light
causes soul fires
conscientious conflagrations

they have placed fire extinguishers
at every corner
waiting to put out fires
which they always imagine
to be furious forest fires

I admit I'm a pyromaniac
when it comes to lighting fires
in other people's hearts and minds
I love to watch from a distance
as their eyes light up
and their souls burn with life

Bearers of Light

Before I Read My Poem

Before I read this poem, I want to tell you some things
about myself.

I know—I'm like you
I can't stand this confessional poetry crap.
The inner recesses of the soul and all that.
I think the more you tell,
the more you hide from others and yourself.
Nietzsche said nobody ever wrote an authentic
autobiography
and I'm not about to prove him wrong.

My life isn't a poem
it's a clearance sale at Wal-Mart
buying all the Easter stuff
at half price
the week after the big rock is supposed
to have been moved from the cave.

While I'm always late for the sales,
I'm always on time for the trivial things in life:
mowing the lawn
picking up the kids up soccer
making sure the bras are snapped before they're placed in
the washer
buying tampons with double coupons.

I always look at my life like I'm a relief pitcher
in the bullpen warming up
waiting and waiting and waiting
inning after inning after inning
for the big moment in the big game
but that big moment in the big game never comes
and all I ever do is warm up
for a great moment that never comes.

Or I'm the kid playing Candy Land
who gets all the way to Ice Cream at the top of the

board
and then selects Candy Canes card
and practically goes back to the beginning.

Mercilessly mundane moments
form a ladder of
endless foreplay in our lives.
They are like ads promoting
the great new abdomen wheel
that is supposed to give you a six pack like
Adonis
but two months after you bought it
ends up in the garage as the replacement
tire
on your wheelbarrow.
They are like holy books
saying the kingdom of God is within you,
but the last time you looked within
yourself
you only found split-level ranch in
Bolingbrook.
They are like the glistening, glamorous
face
on the barstool
at the beginning of evening
that by the end of the evening becomes
a mirage of mascara
as dirty streams drip down her cheeks.
They are like the vociferous promises of
politicians
during the heat of an election
becoming the casual compromises of
diluted legislation.
They are like the beautiful rooms
on Home and Garden television
that you try to emulate,
but end up calling someone to finish for
you.

The big moments of life are not:
when the walls of Jericho tumble
when Haley's Comet sparkles across the sky
when a knockout punch fells a fighter
or when Sisyphus' boulder goes over the hill.

The big moments of life
are not when the boulder clears the ridge
but when we tie our shoes
spit on our hands
take deep breaths
flex our muscles
focus all our energy
and try all over again

realizing
each moment is history
each moment is passion
each action is meaning.

With Big Mac breath
Tide scented clothes
Wal-Mart fanny packs
we can still raise our arms to the heavens
and become heroes
shaking our fists to the gods
(before they strike us down)
and yell
"I have lived, I have lived, I have lived."

And that is the whole meaning of life
to be able to look to the heavens
and scream "I have lived, I have lived"—
to have carved epic lives
from ordinary moments.

This is my life—and your life too
That was my poem—and your poem too.
And you still don't know me
And I still don't know myself.

BEING MARGINALIZED

I

WE EXIST ON THE BORDERS OF THE BOUNTIFUL CORNFIELD. THE FARMERS ALLOWS US TO EXIST SO LONG AS WE DON'T MINGLE WITH HIS PRECIOUS CORN. YOU SEE, WEEDS AREN'T PERMITTED IN FINE FERTILE SOIL.

II

We
Recive
So Few
Nutrients

We
Barely
Survive.

While
Crops Devour

Cavier
Caliber
Dung,

We
Subsit
On
Rocky
Ground.

The
Health
Care
We receive

Pales in
Comparison
With what
Corn gets:

They're
Covered in
Protective
Spray

Warding off
Bugs that
Come to
Live off us.

As you can
Gather our

Self-Esteem
Is not what it
Should be.

Whose would

When all they

Do is curse

And then

Rip us from

The Turf?

III

WITHOUT A CLUE WE ARE ATTACKED: RUN OVER BY LAWN MOWERS, CASTRATED BY CLIPPERS, SMOTHERED BY CHEMICAL WARFARE. WE HAVE NO MEANS FOR REDRESS SINCE WE DON'T BELONG TO THE FERTILE CENTER. THE FARMER HATES US BECAUSE NOBODY WILL BUY US.

IV

We've
Sent
Reps
To the

Field
To Fight
Rights–

None
Returned.

We're
Only
Weeds

We'll
Never
Be Corn.
We
Still

Exist
On the
Edge.
We'

ll
Turn
Yel-
low

And
Brown
And
Perish.

We'
ll
Never
Live

In the
Prom-

Ised
Land
Or

Even

A

Good

Neigh-

Bor-

Hood
Finis.

(At a grocery store where customers bag their own stuff to get extraordinary discounts.)

Are you Italian?
I couldn't remember when I last heard that question.
Are you Italian?
I'm not Italian.
What are you then?
What do I look like?
I'm not sure.
I am a customer in this store.
But what are you?
I'm whatever you think I am.
I've not seen curly hair like yours for such a long time.
You should get out more.
Your nose is interesting too.
Oh, thanks.
Are you Greek?
I am not.
What are you then?
I'm Jewish.
Jewish? There are not many of you down here.
Not any decent bagel places either.
Not a synagogue to be found. No real allies.
You know what I am. But what are you?
That's none of your business. But I'm not of your ilk.
But I told you what I am.
That was your choice, young man.
What are you? Are you Greek or Italian?
I'm not going to say.
May I assume, Ms., you're also a Jew.
I was, am not now, nor will ever be a Jew.
Then how did you know I was a Jew?
Let's just say I'm a census taker for a particular group that likes to know when new people

Census Taker

move in.
I began to remember the curse of her questions.
Sir, you're total is nineteen forty-four.
Go pay your bill, my nice Jewish friend.
What are you going to do with your survey?
You'll find out later.
Sir, the total is nineteen forty-four.
You better pay now. We'll talk later.
When I looked up from writing the check, the census taker
had disintegrated after spinning through the revolving door.
Change in pocket, bags in hand, I suddenly recalled—

Auschwitz, Dachau, and Buchenwald.

The Gray Area
(for Marc Smith)

I

The developer of our neighborhood
Did a strange thing.
He ceded a small gray area
To the twelve residents on our cul-de-sac.

At first, nobody thought twice
About the small gray area.
The soil didn't look rich enough
To support life.

II

It became a place for adolescent smokers
To throw their cigarette butts.
The gray spot became
A garbage grabber.

At last, the neighbors said: "Enough of this.
Let's get rid of that eyesore.
Let's get rid of that place.
Let's plant sod over the gray area."

III

The neighbors sodded and re-sodded
But it wouldn't take.
No matter what they did
It still remained charcoal gray.

One neighbor said
Another seconded
A third echoed:
"We'll sell back the gray spot."

But the developer, who died
Couldn't be reached
And the village had
A gray-spot epidemic all over town.

The neighbors concealed the area with a tarp

But it mysteriously disappeared.
Some say slurped up by the earth.
It disappeared in the grungy gray.

IV

One day on a whim
One of the tiny kids
Sprinkled some tomato seeds
Into the cigarette butted gray area.

The next day fourteen-foot
Tomato plants with fat fresh tomatoes
The size of cantaloupes
Enticed the neighbors.

Within minutes every tomato
Had been plucked from the vines.
The next day tremendous tomatoes
Watermelon-sized hung like milk-heavy breasts.

The neighbors began throwing different seeds
Into the gray area.
Corn, peas, rice, and thyme
Instantaneously grew.

The gray area became sacred ground.
Guards ensured
No cigarette butts incurred
God's gray earth.

V

With each successful harvest
Acrimony invaded.
To whom did the gray area
Truly belong?

The neighbors nearest to it?
The ones who lived in the neighborhood the longest?
The ones whose children first threw the seeds in?
The kids who threw the butts in?

"It's mine," each neighbor asserted.
The gray area is mine."
"We all own the gray area," the only old neighbor replied.
"That's communism, a neighbor hissed."

VI

At the same time the neighbors
Fought for the fertile gray area
People around the globe fought for
Gray areas in their worlds.

They fought for the gray areas by
Fudging, feigning, fraud
Overcharging, underpaying
And skillfully scape-goating.

In each case the more people fought
The more the gray areas expanded
Claiming exceptions, special circumstances,
Emergencies, contingencies, and urgencies.

VII

The blue planet became the gray planet.
Six billion people spoke in thousands of tongues.
With the same refrain:
"The gray areas are mine."

The rain forests are mine
The buffalo are mine
The sweatshops are mine.
The o-zone layer is mine.

At each of those gray areas
A general appeared.
"Those gray spots aren't yours
They're mine,"

The people asked: "Why are they yours?"
"Because I said they were mine.

Because I am bigger than all of you.
Because they're mine.

My Monroe Doctrine says:
God says all the gray spots belong to me.
Since you squabble over who owns the gray spots
Community and caring has gone to the wind.

Without caring and community
I can come and paint the gray areas
Any color I choose
Even a vile shade of green."

VIII

Back in the cul-de-sac
The gray area proved a bounty
The neighbors congregated to it
As if it were fifty percent sale at Wal-Mart.

But one day after each neighbor
Retained an attorney
The great growth shriveled up and died
Nothing would grow in the grungy gray dirt.

Wind-blown corpses of tomatoes, peas, and corn
Flowered neighbors' yards.
Everyone wanted everybody else
To pick the stuff up.

IX

The neighbors figured the one
Who killed the bounty
Would be the guilty conscience
To remove the mess.

When the old man appeared shoveling
En masse, the neighbors approached
"Why did you do it?

Why are you cleaning it up?"

"Yesterday, each of you claimed the area for your own
At the exclusion of others.
Today, I hear 'It's not mine.
Let the general have the gray area.'"

.

"We don't want the gray area any more.
It's the generals to do with as he pleases.
Nothing can grow in it anymore.
There's nothing for us to gain."

X

The old man threw his shovel to the ground:
"We can't give the gray area to the general.
He'll define it with his own colors:
We may not like how it looks."

"Better his colors than gray,"
The neighbors nodded.
"Maybe with a new color
Something will grow there."

"But something else is starting to grow there!"
The old man shouted.
The neighbors looked closely
And couldn't see with their eyes.

"What's growing?" the neighbors wondered.
"The only crop that matters,"
The old man muttered
"The only crop that matters.

"You don't see it yet
But its roots run deep
It's always been there
In the ground by your feet."

The Only Mountain

I

The mountain sticks out of the green plains
It's strange out of there by itself in the flatlands
Thousands and thousands of acres of redundant
corn and wheat fields.

Nobody's ever climbed the mountain
Nobody's been to the top
Nobody's even gotten halfway up

The villagers want the mountain gone
Dynamite it to the ground
"What's the use of it if we can't climb it?"
They want to know.

A village campaign against the mountain finally succeeds.
Proposition two forty-four passes unanimously
Without a single plea or cry
Except from one single sick girl.

II

Mountains are sacred places.
Moses received the Ten Commandments on Mount Sinai
And on Mount Olympus
Zeus, Hera, and company held court.

But in this place these villagers
Want the mountain removed:
Their goals to make to the world a safer place
By making it flat-chested.

Nobody's ever climbed the mountain
Nobody's been to the top
Nobody's even gotten halfway up

III

The single sick girl laments that the mountain
Is a sanctified zone.
God's to create and destroy

Not ours to desecrate.
The single sick girl
In a wheelchair with braces and a permanent frown
Tells the villagers on cable TV:
We need something impossible to keep us awake.
We need dreams to spur us on.
"I want that mountain there simply
because it is impossible to climb it.
I want that mountain there because it's unattainable."

Nobody's ever climbed the mountain
Nobody's been to the top
Nobody's even gotten halfway up

IV

"I want the mountain there because
It's different than all the plains and the fields.
The fields are no different than the same commercial
Being shown over and over again," the little girl says.

Nobody's ever climbed the mountain
Nobody's been to the top
Nobody's even gotten halfway up

"Mountains are to be climbed.
That is all," the mayor meanders.
"If no one can climb them
Then they're going to fall.

"That mountain turns us into failures.
The mountain mocks us with its height.
From the top it ridicules us
And keeps us in our place.

"We're going to turn that mountain
Into a corn field at the edge of
De Santo's farm.
It's going to be as normal as your front
yard."

V

"Isn't there an ordinance that says
Landscapes can't be defaced?" the girl
wonders.
"Isn't the removal of a mountain the same
as
A mastectomy of the earth?"

"Mother Earth is not going to care," the
mayor snorts.
"She's got thousands of mountains ev-
erywhere.
If she loses one of ten thousand breasts
Who the hell is going to care?"

"What about the deer, foxes, and birds
Living on the mountain," the little girl
winces.
"What's going to happen to them
When this one of a kind mountain is
gone?"

VI

"The mountain's one of a kind," the
mayor shouts.
"It's a kind we don't want around here.
The mountain's so tall and so high.
And the high and mighty can't live around
here."

Nobody's ever climbed the mountain
Nobody's been to the top
Nobody's even gotten halfway up

VII

"You can't stand the mountain
Because you can't climb it," the little girl laughs.
"You hate the possibility
That climbing it is an impossibility."

VIII

When the villagers raze the mountain
They are delighted to find
How easily it caves in
Like a house of cards.

"The bigger they are
The harder they fall,"
The villagers hoot.

IX

They live in a community
That never rises to the top.
They have no impossible dreams
Nothing they couldn't do.

They had nothing to climb
They had nothing to say
They had nothing to live for
They had taxes to pay.

Nobody's ever climbed the mountain
Nobody's been to the top
Nobody's even gotten halfway up

Elegies on Education

University Zoo

University zoos are the best ways to domesticate
Radical intellectuals.

Wild-eyed thinkers, missers of appointments who
turn street corners unshaven with old cigarette papers
stuck to smelly jeans with leaves in hair,
become bleary-eyed academics of the new millennium.

At the zoo these pubic bearded radicals
are shaved and retrained.
They are given university posts
where they conform to institutional bars and biases:

jumping through hoops for tenure
flattering phonies for office space
caterwauling for course reductions
elbowing for position at the copy machine
stabbing enemies with gossip
fighting for the last piece of chalk at the blackboard.

They fight each other
for nothing more than
their petty pride
and intellectual hegemony.

If theses radicals went back into the wild
they would never survive.
Their lives are circumscribed
and trivialized—

In universities, radicals are kept in captivity.
Occasionally they roar in classrooms so loud
students believe these animals are dangerous
but they're not—they're just putting on a show.

Ivory Towers

there
are
no
elevators
to
the
top
of
ivory
towers . . .

and no way down
once you get up

Ideals

cultures
viewing
ideals
as
hyperbole
gingerly
gravitate
toward
eons
of
ironic
pirouettes
while
tripping
over
untied
shoelaces

Drill

in hallways we huddled
first graders waiting for the end—
of the world
kneeling on sticky floors
heads between knees
wondering whether our umbilical cords
stretched to heaven
the evil eastern enemy fondling fears
sinister sirens blending with the finality of the
lunch bell
the Angel of Death hovering with a clipboard
doing a preliminary count
teachers' ashen faces cheering us on
oblivion arching over the principal's
pronouncement
this is only a . . .
drill

Holy Space

there's a space
(and it's not a church, temple, or mosque)
that's holier than anything
and should never be defaced
by politics, war, or indifference
and that's the space where
words merge into a tapestry of action
and heart reaches out to heart

My Teacher Hall of Fame

(To be read to one's wife as part of reparation instead of wasting 4 bucks for a Hallmark card.)

As a teacher myself I like to reminisce about the best teachers I've ever had.
I'm sure if you asked Plato he'd say Socrates was his best teacher.
I'm sure if you asked Helen Keller she'd say Anne Sullivan was her best teacher.
I'm sure if you asked 11 of the 12 disciples they'd say Jesus was their best teacher.
I'm sure if you asked 9 out 10 children, they'd say something on television was their best teacher.
When I think of my best teachers, I think of the heavily bearded, pipe-smoking world literature teacher who told us that we shouldn't write down everything he said as gospel but to be selective about what I think about. He taught me Selectivity.
When I think of my best teachers, I think of my father allowing his children to paint an entire wall of the dining room though when they finished it was the antithesis of the Sistine Chapel. He taught me Patience.
When I think of my best teachers, I think of my uncle telling me over and over that I had something special in me. He taught me Faith in Myself.
When I think of my best teachers, I think of my mother. She taught me Family.
When I think of my best teachers, I think of experience. It taught me my Limitations and continues to remind me my Limitations every day.
Why don't I think of you as one of my best teachers?
I guess because you're too close to me, like my own reflection sometimes.
Why don't I think of you as one of my best teachers?
Maybe because you can make me so angry I feel like stabbing you with my harshest words.
Maybe because you are the best scholar of me and know more about me than I do about myself.
Maybe because you know what's in my best interest much better than I do.
Maybe because only my shadow has been with me longer than you have.
You taught me about human suffering, especially yours from moment to moment.
By consensus and I'm afraid as an awkward afterthought
I hereby induct you into my Teacher Hall of Fame.
You deserved to be inducted much earlier, but your political enemies got in the way.
Your biggest political enemy is my Feelings, which you have hurt on more than one occasion.
They're quick to condemn and convict, much slower to promote and praise.
They don't mend quickly and some of the aches, pains, and bruises of twenty years past have formed a pretty strong coalition.
But that coalition compared to the Party of my newly found gratitude is undone.
Thus with the power vested in myself by myself and for myself
I officially induct you, my wife, into my Teacher Hall of Fame.

Suburban Soliloquies

Cul-de-Sac

In our cul-de-sac . . .

The worst thing that happens is
Prairie winds upending portable baskets.

Careful to line up recycling bins
exactly at the curb,
Lawn-mowing legends cut diamonds in the
rough.
Kids whose heads are expanded twice their
size
By heavy-looking helmets
Briskly bike and blade in circles
On the safe circular street
Like dogs chasing their tails.

The perfume of sagaciously seasoned burgers
Confronts the musk of freshly stained decks.
Inchoate apple and peach trees
Braced by stakes
Line up against
A farm destined for commercial chaff.

You see the kids play
And you know you've
Done the right thing
Living in the cul-de-sac
It's as sterile as an alcohol drenched cotton
ball
But sterility is safe for kids
And that's what matters.
They can run, jump, and live
While we finish our basements.

Our little DNAs
Live effortlessly and blindly
The best way to live
As we worry about mortgage payments,
Life insurance, and college IRAs.
In the cul-de-sac

Parents resemble the living young
Who love the humidity and the sun.
But even in suburban despair
We've still got cable
(And wallets filled with golden plastic
Make our budgets egregiously elastic.)

From the cul-de-sac
Kids aren't going to have any of the big scars
Slit their wrists
Prove to the whole world why they're right
And everyone else is wrong.

No brilliantly defined sphere
Commands the sunset
Above the cul-de-sac.
Ribbons of pinkish-orange haze lay laconically
On slanted silent roofs.

This is the innocence we have captured.
This is the childhood we wish we all had.
This is the childhood of our children.
This is the keyhole where we live.

Four farms one after the other
Lead to the end of my world
Where sky and earth pretend to meet
Where eternity emerges for me.

But eternity like any ware in our village
Can be bought and sold
And my farmer neighbors have done just that
Exchanged their farms to the rhetoric of progress
For business parks, duplexes, strip malls,
(And probably a children's petting zoo).

Can I blame them?
I have a family too.
Two little girls
Two college educations
On the horizon.
Yet the farmers haven't just sold
One thousand acres of ruddy land,
They've sold a gateway to eternity.

My eye is led along the top of corn stalks
Past distant trees and fields
Swallowed by the inverted blue ocean
Toward the end of all that I can see.

You put parts of the past in museums
But no museum can capture my view of eternity.
In ten years
All I'll be able to see
Is a blown-up picture
Of what once was eternity.

Cornered by a complex
Of townhouses and homes
Decks, duplexes, town homes, fortressed fences
Grassy stalls of land
With embryonic and fledgling trees,

The Long View of Life

I can look up, but that isn't the same.
The sky is just a ceiling
My paintbrush can't reach
Its majesty depleted
Without the earth running up to greet it.

The night sky also loses its luster
Looking up as if from a canister
Up a tube
At a parcel of stars.
I can crane my neck
Or lie on my back
And see thousands of stars.
Yet I can't see the hypothetical point
Where sky and earth meet.

The village and mayor and progress
Have robbed me of
More than gorgeous view.
They have robbed me of the long view of life.

I will never dream the same way
Without a runway to eternity.
Where sky and earth meet
The dreams of humanity
Become complete.

The long view of life
Is four fertile farms
Stretching to eternity.
You can see forever.
You can imagine forever.
You realize that progress is regress
Otherwise named.

Sensual Winds

Perky
Winds
Curled
Between
Buttons
Of
My
Shirt
Undressing
Me
In
Front
Of
The
Hubris
Of
The
High
Heavenly
Moon.

Passive
Resistance
To
Sheets
Of
Rain

Means
Cold
Currents
Rushing
Down
Facial
Canals.

Passive Resistance

(Written by the Only Teenager in the Cul-de-Sac.)

In the right light, the paint may look good.
But in this light—

I'd worship light to get the right kind
For example, the sun.
But the sun is no longer the right light.

In the right light, my life may look good.
But as it is, I've not found that light yet.

In the right light, my face may look good.

In the right light I might look good to someone
He/She/They/It

What if I'm never able to find the right light?
Whether I look to others or inwardly.
What if the light is always diffuse
Never focused on me properly?

In the Right Light

Solid
Sunshine
Prohibited
The
Usual
View
Of
The
Red
Barn
And
His
Heathen
Hands
Converting
Life
To
Dinner.

Untitled

Tender Tirades

O! Blessed Pergo

O! Blessed Pergo
Thank you for entering our lives.
O! Flooring of laminate floorings
Thank you for listening to our cries.

We could not live without you.
Our lives are a series
Of spills, stains, and spots.
The miracle of you
Is how easily
You are resurrected
When evil matter
Attacks you.

Everything
Even myrrh and frankincense
Wipes up
(Hallelujah!)
With a damp rag
No lingering spots or rings.

Sloppy people of the world
Rejoice! Rejoice!
We can spill as much as we want
On our laminate deity.
Our resilient savior
Repels satanic filth.

The day of reckoning is upon
The rest of the carpet-covered earth.
A great flood of mustard and grape juice
Will descend upon
Every so-called repellant fiber.
Find faith in pergo
Before the apocalypse
Blessed are they who
Walk on thy divine face.
Find faith in laminate flooring
Find your earthly bliss.

Untrained Dogs

The black Labrador is dainty
About her toilet etiquette
Whining and wiggling
Nudging my arm with wet nose
Declaring her purpose
Hitting the brown spot on the lawn
Like a heat-seeking missile.

But the other dog. . . .

The other dog is an anarchist
An excremental experimenter
With existential irony.

It upsets the fleeting order
Of our quasi-dysfunctional home
When we find the results
Of his anarchy
Distributed around the house
As wealth should be.

The dog slips away
From our television-weary eyes
To explore the four corners
Of the house.

The sharp stench of Clorox
The salve of often-attacked white carpet
Brings tears to our eyes.

The anarchist dog
Wags his tail
In the face
Of sharp cruel words
Wild waving hands
And promises of deportation.

He knows he'll receive absolution
Even if he doesn't repent
We'll always love him
Above the vile stench.

Majority Rules

Each time I lined up my text
One line jumped out of place.

For hours, days, and weeks
I tried to line up the text in which
One line jumped out of place.

I backspaced the line
Even deleted it and re-pasted still
One line jumped out of place.

I turned the computer off
I turned the computer on yet
One line jumped out of place.

I even tried the least helpful of computer aids:
The Help Button behold
One line jumped out of place.

Everything on the page
Lined up the way it should except
One line jumped out of place.

I couldn't stand
I abhorred the obstreperous insolence as
One line jumped out of place.

It wasn't right.
It upset the harmony of my document that
One line jumped out of place.

With indignation and humiliation
I rebooted and called support services but predictably
One line jumped out of place.

Finally, a scenario I had not thought of emerged.
After striking a series of wrong buttons I saw
Those other thirty lines were out of place.

Contritely and obediently
They jumped over and lined up under
The only line in the right place.

Flattery

I
I never was a good flatterer
That's why I always left bars
Angry and empty-handed.

I was never any good at buttering up
(Maybe that's why Menelaus
Lost Helen to Paris)

II
She could flatter the sun to shine
The wind to blow
The flowers to bloom
And me to do anything she wanted.

Her flattery caressed
My spiritual G-Spot.

She flattered
And got everything
I didn't
And got nothing.

III
I hated flattery
Thought it a bribe
Telling people
What they wanted to hear.

People devour flattery
Like cheap chocolates
Growing fat from
Syrupy compliments
Expecting feasts of flattery
Wherever they go.

In their suppliant eyes
In their expectant grins
Necks craning

To hear the good word.

III
But I am not the Gospel
I have no Good Gooey Words.

Why do they need me so?
Why do they need me to feed their egos.
I would rather feed the world
Than feed their egos.

Why must I fill their spirits
With light and warmth?

IV
I was above flattery
Rejected flattery.

She flattered
And got everything
I didn't
And got nothing.

V
Then I learned to look and listen. . . .

VI
I flattered so much
That at first
It hurt like doing
Two hundred abdominal crunches
After dinner.

VII
I told her she had a beautiful face
And her face became beautiful.

I told her she had a beautiful voice
And her voice became beautiful.

I told her she was beautiful
In everything she did

And I found beauty
Everywhere she was.

VIII
I flattered the sun
And it shone for me.
I flattered the flowers
And they bloomed for me.
I flattered myself
And I finally became
Bearable for me.

Children of Kosen-Rufu

Doves and Gold

(On the occasion of the official opening of Soka University of America, 3 May 2001.)

From wood boxes stacked near the Peace Fountain
Doves soar into the blue sky
On a miraculous May afternoon.
Theirs is not a flight of fancy—

Before, they rushed here, to California
To exhume gold nuggets
From the belly of the earth.
Today, they rush to this new capital of peace
On the summit
Of a new century
For a new way of being human,
Not for fool's gold.

Squadrons of doves
Twirl on winds.
Each surrounding mountaintop a torch holder
For beacons of peace—

That is what the hopeful longing
Of the people on the summitt see.
Each valley is a corridor of hope
A passageway transforming

What they see in their hearts
Is the flight of the doves
On the winds of peace
Winds they remember to dream
Winds they set in motion.

Eyes

In my daughter's
onerous eyes
I see the eyes of all children
troubled
gentle
searching
terrified
hungry
angry
dying—
eyes

Making War

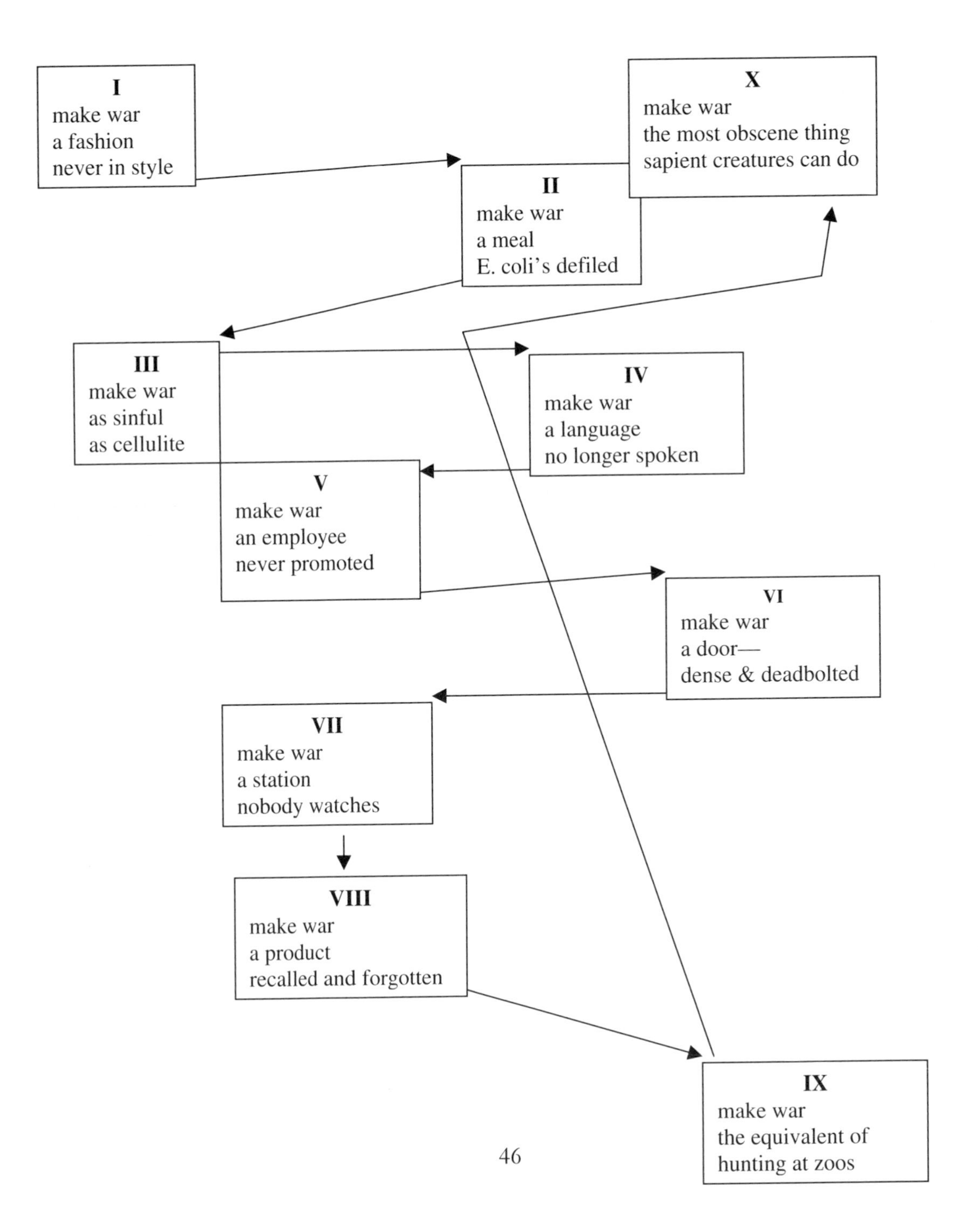
I
make war
a fashion
never in style
II
make war
a meal
E. coli's defiled
III
make war
as sinful
as cellulite
IV
make war
a language
no longer spoken
V
make war
an employee
never promoted
VI
make war
a door—
dense & deadbolted
VII
make war
a station
nobody watches
VIII
make war
a product
recalled and forgotten
IX
make war
the equivalent of
hunting at zoos
X
make war
the most obscene thing
sapient creatures can do

Thousands of Reasons

In a library with thousands of books
The scholar should find thousands of reasons to hope.

Beside a fireplace with her lover
She should find thousands of reasons to hope.

In a garden amid dozens of red, yellow, and white roses
We should find thousands of reasons to hope.

In a classroom with bright-eyed students
The teacher should find thousands of reasons to hope.

In a sea of summer sunlight
The swimmers should find thousands of reasons to hope.

In vast rivers of deep meditation
The yogi should find thousands of reasons to hope.

In front of a palette of possibilities
The painter should find thousands of reasons to hope.

In the grocery store with four annoying but lovable kids
The father should have find thousands of reasons to hope.

On a mountaintop with a view of other mountaintops
She should find thousands of reasons to hope.

Seeing a half-open door, staircase, or exit sign
We should find thousands of reasons to hope.

When other people keep their promises
We should find thousands of reasons to hope.

Watching people work and play together
We should find thousands of reasons to hope.

In the revelation that life cannot go on without hope
We should find thousands of reasons to hope.

Inner Revolution

(for SGI)

I can see your inner revolution even though you think I can't.
I have seen how your sloped shoulders are now square.
I have seen how you sit straight and not slouch in the chair.
I have seen bounce and confidence in your stride.
I have seen the light and determination in your eyes.
I have seen the utmost courtesy when you drive.
I have seen you speak to braggarts with respect.
I have seen you flex your muscles as you breathe.
I have seen you mend what you've done and do what you thought you couldn't.
I have seen you embrace the mantle of uncertainty.
I have seen you fell the tree with one sharp swing of an ax.
I have seen you be patient with fools.
I have seen you reach out your hand without balling the other in the fist.
I have seen you take a bullet in head without grimacing.
I have seen you run in delight and not in fright.
I have seen you shoulder great weight without a grunt or a groan.
I have seen you build up others when you could.
I have seen you help the homeless with the heart of a saint.
I have seen you grin without a hint of despair.
I have seen you make a basket without looking at the rim.
I have seen you play in your work and work at your play.
I have seen you happy in what is and is not known.
I have seen you live everyday unburdened by sin.
I have seen you dance like leaf on a windy day.
I have seen you jump like cat from a counter.
I have seen you smile at the play of children.
I have seen you swim and smile and glide and grin.
I have seen you hug people for their sake and not yours.
I have seen you climb mountains without complaint.
I have seen you sleep in peace and wake with vitality.
I have seen you sail in the wind.
I have seen you stare at the horizon and not peek over your shoulder.
I have seen you turn rumors and catcalls into knowledge and wisdom.
I have seen you build a life from a shack to a cathedral.
I have seen your inner revolution.

Metaphysical Mischief

All Sales Are Final

take it back
we can't
take it back
we can't. once the cat's out of the hat, the genie out of the bottle, hope is out of the box it's yours
take it back: here's the receipt, I've even underlined the item
all sales are final—receipts don't matter
we bought it a half hour ago
time doesn't matter to us
it's ripped and the wrong size and the wrong color
it's yours
you can give me a store credit for it
no store credit—all sales are final
then I want to exchange this item for another
that's not possible
you have 43 aisles, thousands of shelves, and millions of items in this store
but not one exactly like you bought
you mean I can't exchange this for something else
not in this store. now if you buy other stores, then you'll have to deal with their policies, but in this store once you've bought it you've bought it
where did this silly philosophy come from
this silly philosophy as you call it is part of the collective wisdom of our board of trustees. they believe that once you've committed yourself to buying anything in our store, it's your forever. all sales are final. you've made a decision to purchase an item. it is yours. live with it
if I can't get my money back, I'll just leave it here, on the counter. I don't want your merchandise. and I'm going to tell all my friends not to shop at this store
we can't take the merchandise back under any circumstances
idiot, I don't want it either. it's going the trashcan outside
we can't allow you to do that. you've bought, so you keep it
if I stuff it in the trashcan outside, who's going to know
we will know. you bought the item, you bought so you're going to have to keep it
I can't dump this anywhere I want to dump it. I'll throw it out the car window
and if you do, we will make sure that you get it back
what is the matter with you? I don't want it. I'm just going to throw it away like a disposable razor when I get home

we'll send you another one in the mail
you won't know when I get rid of it
ma'am, you'd be surprised how much we know. it wouldn't be wise for you to get rid of it
this thing is not going with me out of the store. here on this counter it's going to stay
then I'm going to have to call security, ma'am, because all sales are final. around here people take responsibility
for their shopping, what they buy they keep
I'm never shopping here again. there are plenty of stores everywhere
but only one like ours where you have to choose like it's the end of the world, where everything matters on each
purchase, where what you buy is yours and yours forever
I won't ever shop here again
you have to shop here because what you want you can't get anywhere else
and you know that and take advantage of your customers
we don't like to put it that way, ma'am, but we'll put it in another
all sales are final

Incredulous Intersection

At the intersection of Backway and Frontier Roads
A red Lexus pretentiously, rudely, uncivilly, uncouthly, indecently
Cut in the front of me without acknowledging that without my courtesy
It could have never made the turn.
That car had no right to be there:
The light had already changed from yellow to red
Ten seconds earlier.
After the light had changed, I graciously allowed two vehicles
(a mom-manned mini-van and an illegal alien's pick-up truck) to turn.
But I refused the third by inching up into the intersection
A warning to the red Lexus my graciousness was at an end
To back up, back off, go back, and let me go.
The Lexus merely gleamed its teeth at me
Made a hairpin turn inches from my bumper
Screeching tires laughing and leering
Then sped down the road.
The driver never even waved to me to say: Thanks.
More than the mobile status symbol,
This made my adrenaline jump off the scale.

I could have let it go
Slide off my shoulders
Turned on to the highway exit fifty yards away
Headed toward the meadows and cheese of Door County.

But when people wrong us
They hatchet our hearts
Hurry us from our humanity and our better good
Sautee our souls in sauces of fury.
Throw left brain and right brain into civil war.
My adrenaline encouraged me to hunt down the red Lexus like a Nazi war criminal.
Then it would see the wrath of Achilles or at least some 21st century facsimile.
Even though I didn't know precisely what I'd do
(It might range from impalement to a haughty football victory dance over a fallen player)
I didn't know, but someone would pay
Pay more than the mom of the mom-manned mini-van paid for her leopard-skinned seat covers at Wal-Mart.

At first the bend in the road, the Home Depot, and the fiery twilight concealed the red Lexus from the rush of adrenaline that guided my eyes.
It disappeared in dense suburban sprawl
Behind the Red Lobsters, Bakers Squares, Walgreens, Wal-Marts, and Marshalls.

Yet for an instant and only an instant I thought I saw the car between the picture frame created by the Home Depot and Marshalls.
Because of what I thought I saw
My foot and gas pedal became one with floor.

You always think you're gaining.
You always do
Eventually I'd catch the red Lexus.
I'd run it off the road near the Amoco on 135th street
Or maybe it would stumble on the part of Frontage Road that dead-ends.
I never lost sight but never gained.
The smoked glass windows wouldn't let me see inside to
The Naperville Bushman Viagra-addict dotcommer
With a half million dollar cavern resting on an eighth of an acre lot.

After a trek through suburban sprawl and several parking lots at malls,
I entered a dark junkyard of rusty hoods, dented doors, cracked windshields,
Slashed leather seats, headlights like detached eyeballs, steering wheels, hubcaps, sparkplugs, mufflers, and the intestines of cars, and mosquito tribes in their condominium tires, hills of discarded cars nobody would ever want to climb.

Maybe it wasn't even the same car I started chasing.
Maybe I shouldn't have come so far out of my way.
The red light on the oil gauge
Shouts at me that to look at the coupon on the dashboard for ten dollars off at Jiffy Lube. My weak-sighted headlights tell me my battery is going too.
Miles and miles from the intersection of Backway and Frontier Roads
In the beginning . . .
If I had just ignored the car
Forced my adrenaline to quell.
If I stopped at Bakers Square instead and eaten a lemon meringue pie
Negotiated a settlement of my cerebellum civil war
I wouldn't be lost the junk pile of cars
Waiting for the guy from the commercial
"Hey, that old car is worth money"
To show up and pull the door off my car.

Many of the rusty car carcasses looked familiar to me
Like dead relatives down the bright corridor when we die.
No!

They all look like every single car that had done me wrong:
Cut in front of me, flipped me off, didn't appreciate my letting them in when they would have sat at that corner forever. Ungrateful bastards!
Yes, in this junkyard I see all the wrongdoers from my life.
They don't look exactly as I remember them though
They look like they want to be left in peace to die
But all I want to resurrect and then destroy them again and again.
They aren't good enough to let die a natural death rusting in the rustic rain.
They need to be slain!

Adrenaline once again agitated my eyes to relentlessly to examine each pile if need be the case and find that red Lexus.
The wheels clattered over clumps of car guts as I wound around each pile until I found the guilty party. At last I found my prey.
This couldn't be the car. It shook as if from fear or palsy.
It was the same car, but not a Lexus.
It wasn't a Rolls Royce, Cadillac, or even a Lincoln.
It wasn't even a mid-sized luxury family sedan that got 18 miles in the city and 24 on the highway.
It was just an old red Gremlin from the 1970s. And nobody was inside. Nobody. Not the Naperville Bushman Viagra-addicted dotcommer
With a half million dollar cavern resting on an eighth of an acre lot. Nobody.

What a waste!
My car rusting in a junkyard with the
Damn battery on its last legs
Lights fading
Air vents exuding faint heat
Numbing night sky
Empty stomach and gas tank, headlight eyeballs looking me up and down with contempt.
All for a Gremlin.
Why did I care that it pretentiously, rudely, uncivilly, uncouthly, indecently
Cut in the front of me? What did it matter?

Only now did it matter
Since I was now here.

A New Method (Based on a near death experience. I could only overhear the following conversation.)

We have a new method up here.

What's that?

God doesn't judge you anymore:
God doesn't give grades.

What? I assumed this would be
a pass/fail situation.

That's not the way we do it now.
You give yourself a grade.

You mean I went through life
looking up at the heavens,
worrying about the Ten Commandments,
and the Sermon on the Mount,
and now you're telling me I have to judge myself?

You seem to understand.

I didn't lie.
I didn't steal.
I didn't covet my neighbor's wife
(Although nobody really coveted her).
I didn't even smoke in No Smoking areas.

Give yourself a grade then.

I want a grade from God.

God's not going to give you one.

I demand it.

We won't accommodate your wishes.

Are you saying that
if I say have lived a good life,

I will go to eternal Club Med?

That's what we're saying.

This is absurd.

My whole life is ludicrous and meaningless
if God can't judge me.

God doesn't judge. He wants you to.

Then I'm just going to say
that I've lived a good life
and then you'll just let me in.

Then we wish to welcome you.

Do you mean to say that anyone who says
"I've lived a good life"
gets in here?

That's the policy.

You mean if Hitler comes here and says
"I've lived a good life,"
then he gets in.

He's here.

That's disgusting.
Heaven with Hitler?
I'm appalled.
Look, I've put in all this time trying to be a good person.
I've lived by God's rules, while others didn't.
I paid attention to them, while others didn't.

So judge yourself on that basis.

I don't know how to judge myself.

You must judge yourself.

What's the point of this place
If I have to judge myself?

You must judge yourself.

This is what I get for following God's rules.
I listened to God.

But did you listen to yourself?

Myself?
What am I an authority on?

You. Your own life.

Myself?
What do I know?

Did you ever listen to yourself? Did you ever look inside?

I never did.

Why not?

When I looked inside I couldn't see because it was so foggy I couldn't see.
When I tried to listen, I couldn't hear anything, not even a peep.

You can't judge yourself then?

No.

We can't allow you in here unless you have looked and listen in here.

I can't.

Then we can't.

God, please judge me.
Please judge me.
Say anything at all.
Tell me I'm the worst person on this planet.
Please tell me the value of my life.

My Gentle Father (an androgynous poem)

I

Ginny Wilson was never the same after she caught her father in bed with the fourth grade teacher, Mrs. Hopper.
When I caught Dad in bed with a student from one of his adult ed classes, I couldn't have been happier.

II

Like clockwork, every three or four years Dad had a nervous breakdown. Mom called them phases. I now know better. They were breakdowns.
Last year Mom left him when he went through his final stage.

III

Before I turned thirteen, I identified four stages.
After a far less deserving colleague received a teaching position,
Dad cried for two days straight. I was only two. He spent four months watching Clint Eastwood and Charles Bronson movies.
His favorite was *Death Wish*, which I remember watching over and over again.
Stage One.
After he found out Mom cheated on him, he cut his bushy hair so short you could see patches of his scalp.
Every other day he had his hair cut. This lasted six months.
Stage Two.
During one month, I fell prey to focalized seizures and my then six-year-old sister Rosalyn had an ovary surgically removed, he would not leave us alone.
He had another line installed in his study and phones put in Rosalyn's and my rooms.
He incessantly called us to make sure we were okay. This lasted a year.
Stage Three.
After receiving a national teaching award, his colleagues ridiculed and ostracized him, even though in his acceptance speech he credited his success to being at an institution with great teachers
(A lie! Dad was head and shoulders above them: he could connect with anyone.).
Stage Four

IV

Dad had one big problem: a huge superego.
In the same way John Holmes had the largest penis I had ever seen, my father had the biggest superego (I'm not one of those females who pretends to overlook that part of a guy's anatomy). He cared about the feelings of everybody. Dad couldn't hurt anyone. Not even his enemies.
That was his problem. Gentle and generous, he never schemed to harm others.
Lucifer would have never fallen from grace were Dad God.
Dad would never dehumanize anyone, even a demon wanting to take his place.
The "worst" thing I ever saw him do was grab and shake a big candy machine until the Starburst I had paid for fell out.

He only resorted to this violence after I we had spent 15 minutes trying to get our money back.

He shook the machine so hard that licorice, M & Ms, Snickers, and Three Musketeers also fell out.

"What should I do with this other candy?" I asked.

"Don't worry about it," he said.

I was a little shocked.

A week later, looking at the outgoing mail, I noticed a check made out to the vendors.

V

I just never met anybody like him.

He understood me.

I could tell him anything.

When I was twelve, I woke up in a pool of blood.

I just lay there in my new canopy bed, glazed-eyed and horrified. I looked like I had been shot. Several huge bloody splotches stained my ET sheets.

Mom, a deep sleeper, couldn't hear. Dad, a light sleeper, did.

"What's the matter, honey?"

I think most girls would shy away from telling their father about their first period. But I knew Dad would understand.

"I ruined my ET blanket," I cried.

After we removed, the blanket and sheet, we discovered that blood had seeped through to the Sealy Postropedic mattress Mom revered.

"Mom's going to kill me. I ruined my new bed. She told I should start wearing tampons. But I forgot."

"This is natural and you have nothing to be ashamed of," Dad said. "Forget about it."

He washed the bloody spots out with a brush and small amount of Clorox. Then he jammed everything into the washer. With two hours to kill, we watched tv. *Death Wish* was on the late show. When a look of despondency or shame came over my face, Dad told me to forget about it. About four a.m., he tucked me into my warm, clean bed. Mom never found out.

VI

Mom took full advantage of Dad's superego. When she wanted something, she laid a guilt trip on him.

"I never had a nice house when I grew up."

Mom grew up poor and in a large family.

She made up for it when she became an adult.

She wanted the big house.

On a professor's salary, Dad couldn't do it unless he became a teaching machine, doing overloads at every community college in a fifty-mile radius.

Lots of courses on leadership with students not much younger than Dad.

Dad bought Mom a nice white house facing a farm.

Mom complained that the glass ceiling. "I can never make as much as you can because I'm a woman."

If she couldn't make as much as he could, then that difference had to come out of someone's hide:

Dad's.

Mom made the budget so she could buy what she wanted and Dad couldn't. Dad only wanted a few dollars a week to buy pop. "The little things like your grape pop add up," she told him, even after going on shopping sprees spending thousands of dollars. My mother constantly took advantage of him and eventually cheated on him.

I suspected something was going on when Mom repeatedly instructed Dad: "Never call me at work. It embarrasses me."

Eventually Dad found about Mom. An anonymous phone call from—as I later discovered from Ginny Wilson—from Ginny's mother, who worked with Mom.

Dad blamed himself.

"Maybe I'm not that good in bed. Maybe I'm not affectionate enough to her. I'll have to change. I'm obviously not meeting her needs."

Mom knew he'd never leave, even after he found out.

She had him over a barrel.

She knew Dad knew that Rosalyn and I loved her.

Since he had such a deep commitment to our happiness, he'd never break up the family. Mom fucked with Dad's superego.

She never had sex with him.

You could tell. He never woke up whistling or singing.

Unnaturally stooped over for a man of 50, he looked down at his Nikes and never at in anybody's eyes.

He murmured when he spoke.

At some point, I believed, he wouldn't be able to take it any more.

VII

For 25 years he grinned and bore it.

He sympathized with her plight as a female banging her head on glass ceilings.

He sympathized with her plight growing up poor.

He sympathized with her plight being married to a loser like him.

He didn't want to hurt the poor thing any more.

Last June, I drove in from the city to surprise Dad.

My last class was cancelled because of reconstruction. Maybe we'd go a movie and then get some ice cream.

He was so down.

Mom had gone to work long ago.

As I pulled up, I saw the expensive roses and rows of freshly planted peach, pear, and pine trees Dad paid for with his blood.

He would always be enslaved.

Something was wrong.

Something was terribly wrong.

Dad usually kept the blinds of upstairs study open.

Sealed shut off the soggy grass and run-off on the driveway were any indications, the sprinklers had been on for hours.
Two rancid recycling bins sat on the curb (Mom programmed Dad to bring them as soon they had emptied them).
Next door, two dogs barked wildly and clawed each other.
Something horrible had happened.
He had gone into another phase, the final phase.
I wondered how he did it: overdose, slit wrists, bullet, hanging?
I had expected this for a long time.
When I found the body, I didn't want to be one of those hysterical women.
I'd go quietly into the house, locate the body, check for vital signs, and then call 911.
Then I'd call Mom and tell her to get her ass back home.
I let myself in the front door with my key.
I wondered where he did it.
Probably not the new leather couch in the family room.
That would be too hard for Mom to clean up.
Sensitive to the end.
As I wandered into the foyer and stuck my head in the dining room and living room, I hoped Mom would feel guilty as hell.
Dad let her do this to him, but she shouldn't have done it.
Not downstairs.
He wouldn't do it in my old bedroom.
Ten to one, he did it in his bathroom.
I tiptoed up the stairs and saw that his bedroom door was cracked. I heard nothing.
I stood fifteen feet from the door, admiring photos of Rosalyn and me on the wall. Suddenly,
I didn't want to go in.
I loved that man.
He couldn't be dead.
I walked back down the stairs.
I'd call Mom and tell her to get home.
Let her be the first one to see him.
Let her. I picked up the blue portable phone in kitchen.
When Mom answered, I hung up.
"I want to see him first," I decided.
"Back up the steps," I said with a determined pace.
I slowly approached the bedroom door.
Thinking him dead, I didn't want to barge right in. Maybe he just overdosed on sleeping bills.
Maybe he's dead on the bed. I'll just peek in.

VIII

I peeked in.

The woman wasn't bad looking.
Leather-faced and a little leather-lunged, a single breast attached to a nice body.
I wasn't appalled and I won't be scarred.
Finally, Dad did something unsaintly.
Finally, he was no longer purely superego.

IX

I never knew Harriett Hopper had a mastectomy.

X

I couldn't wait to tell Ginny Wilson.
She was never going to be the same.
Mom sure wasn't.

Funereal Fragments

In prayer before the electronic ark
I flip through thousands of possibilities:
I can order food
and when I get too fat
can order exercise equipment
and when I get too wrinkled
from tanning under ultraviolet lamps
I can order wrinkle cream
and when my sex drive stalls
I can order pills to tune it up
and when my body sprouts into a hairy rain forest
deforestation can occur in a few fleet moments
and when my eye sight grows dim
my eyes can be surgically saved
and after blinking my surgically altered eyes
I can order anything I want
but the more I order
the hungrier I get.
There's something in the pit of the stomach
something cocked and coiled
an excrutiating hunger
an unquenched thirst
once I get something
it always disappoints me.
I have a spiritual tapeworm
a beast that cannot be satisfied
growing up when my father praised my brother
all I got was nice job
when the crowd roars, does the player know ovations die in the wind?
I wake up everyday waiting to get into a fast car
only to find the tires are flat.
The 8 wonders of the world are overrated
the pyramids are only glorified triangles.
If I had been a contemporary of Christ
I would have come in just a little late for the miracles
Jesus would have been walking on water for 45 minutes
and just when I'd show up they'd say he was through for the day.
I'm in the mood for mountains
and all I get are subatomic particles.

I. Hunger

I am reminded of Heisenberg's Uncertainty Principle:
if you predict place, you can't predict momentum
and if you predict momentum, you can't predict place
this applies precisely to appetite.
If I see what I want, then the momentum pushes the desire away from me
if I try to control the momentum, then the desire cannot predicted
more is never enough.
When I was on the road
everything was parallel to me
everything missed me
but now I can open my jaw like a snake
and everything falls into it
I crave experience, want to know what it's like to be female praying mantis after sex
want to know what it's like to be the pope on the potty
want to know what it's like to be Alexander the Great and have nothing left to conquer
I want to be . . .
everything . . . everywhere . . .
what happens after we die?
the question gnaws at me
It kills me not to know, not to have the answers.
The more and more and more means less and less and less
once you've devoured everything
you realize you've been devoured yourself
swallowed whole by your hunger
St. Anselm says you can't think of a being greater than God,
for God is the most perfect being;
but in my mind there is an even more perfect position
and that is what I want.
Greed is greater than God.

II. Hell

The five-o'clock traffic jam leaves me paralyzed.
Condensed on the four-lane superhighway
inch by inch my car edges forward
and eventually I will be home
sitting in front of theTV
playing the remote control like a classical pianist.
But eventually feels like eons here in the car
in the same sense if I lived millions of years ago
and somebody said "Eventually after the Ice Age
this will be the Grand Canyon."
Eventually my twenty-mile trek will end
but by that time I will have evolved into homo desponditis.
Four parallel lanes run rigidly toward the horizon
into the loud angry rays of the red bellicose sun.
I could kill myself for not leaving earlier
for not leaving my desk messy
and beating the traffic.
Five minutes would have made all the difference in the world.
But once again I sabotaged myself
reorganizing the fax, monitor, layers of papers
and answering one last phone call
condemned my lungs to
sucking up the cumulative exhaust of Henry Ford's legacy,
for three hours
and craving a heaping of pure oxygen.
It would be one thing if I could put the car on Stop
shift my seat into a reclining position
and snore into oblivion—
It's quite another to be ever vigilant
hip-hopping from gas pedal to brake.
Through smudgy smeared salt-covered windows
the sun pours into my eyes
like knives to the eyes after a night of hard drinking
while the latest traffic report from the
All News Station
predicting an extended commute
due to an overturned semi-trailer
tightens the seat belt around my waist
and slurs my anticipation
for the end of this journey.
The styrofoam cup in the half-broken cup holder
contains cold muddy sediments of morning ambrosia

while on the passenger seat
headlines from *The Sun-Times*
announcing more downsizing in my company
wail like wolves whose legs are caught
in sharp inescapable traps.
My life is spent waiting—
waiting for this traffic jam to dissipate
waiting for winter to turn into spring
waiting until just the right job becomes available
waiting for people to value me the way I value myself
waiting for coal to turn into diamonds
waiting for a savior who can't tell time.
As I wait I become a bundle of nervous mannerisms:
cracking my knuckles until they can't be cracked anymore
excavating my nose
biting layers and layers off my nails
locking and unlocking the power locks
resetting the odometer every 10th of a mille
blasting the heater and then the air conditioner
looking in the rear view mirror
and seeing a thousand other cars like my own....
Under the crushing weight of despair
hope is herniated
without hope
what can be done in the world?
what rock can be moved
mountain climbed
problem solved?
I cannot do anything without hope—
Time itself comes to standstill without hope
as the future withers and dies before my eyes.
Hope is like a messenger from the future
that informs me that things are possible there.
But that messenger of the future is pressed under
a great boulder of despair and is smothered.
Despair murders the messenger from the future
despair resists all changes.
What is at rest stays at rest
and rests in peace....
Can't see where I'm driving my car
can't see straight
can't see whether I'm doing a vasectomy or hysterectomy
can't see whether I'm right or wrong
can't see the difference between the heavens and the earth
can't see the difference between good and evil

can't see the difference between my ass and a hole in the ground
can't see the difference
it's like a telescope unable to focus on the stars
a microscope unable to focus on bacteria
can't figure out which exit to get off of
just stuck in this one place
creeping along like a slug
head ready to explode like a supernova
living in an opaquely ocular igloo of invulnerability
have a vendetta against the whole earth
against life, against my parents for conceiving me
for God for birthing the universe.
I have no use for anybody or anything
I just want everything to bend to my will
I want a rainbow over my head all the time
let me get rid of this Christmas garbage
let me find a dumpster for it
I can't believe it all turned out this way
bare trees purple feelings ripe clouds
dripping vile symmetry over the land
cramming cream of wheat down my throat
there are only possibilities for destruction
how different am I than a mosquito
a plant, an amoeba?
how different is my life from any other
if I stopped being angry at the world
what would remain?
If I subtracted my rage from the world, what would be left?
I wish I could live underground like a mole
and never come up and see the light
but even underground there's traffic.
Do you know who I am?
I'm the guy at the top of the hill who pushes the boulder
back down on Sissyphus
silly man if he thinks he's ever going to push anything over on me....
The world's tilted away from me
it's always winter solstice and I'm in the wrong hemisphere
blue Buick in my rearview mirror
inching up
you're too close
I don't like things too close
I like the fact that the earth is 93 million miles from the sun
that's about the right distance
if other people could stay that far away I'd be fine
bumper basher watch out

I'm like the sun
you get too near me and you burn
you have no right to be on the same road with me
this is my road
a road that should have been named after ME not a dead president
or a guy who has kicked back money to the mayor
everybody thinks you owe them
they smile at you and you're supposed to smile back
they do something for you and you're supposed to say thank you.
Two hours in a car
two hours listening to the voices on radio
seeing the same cars in front in back on the side of me
inhaling the same carbon monoxide
thinking the same thoughts.
I've not been able to shake my thoughts
I've never changed my mind about people
the difference between myself and others
is that I know that I'm angry
they're just faking it
who wouldn't be mad in the middle of a traffic jam
it's like having your arms and legs tied
or amputated
it's maddening to see a naked woman on a bed
and you look down and see you don't have a penis
Being angry for so long makes you dizzy
you begin seeing double
you get headaches
you shout and shiver
your blood boils so much that your feelings evaporate at some point
and when your feelings evaporate,
When haven't I been pissed off?
I dream only in red and sometimes white....
Nothing's more dangerous than a wounded animal
I am parallel to everything
parallel lines never meet
I envy perpendicular people
people intersect with others
I just keep on traveling in space and time on my own path
not intersecting with anyone else
parallel, only hitting the world with my anger
never striking it with love
but with the full force of vituperation
I am like an ax that only hits tree stems.
Life bothers me because it always has to have more
it just can't stand still

I regard any space I want as my space.
All the ramps closed until I get near home
only one way to get off and that's twenty miles down the road.
Blood shot sun limping on the horizon
pretending to be king of the planet
you are a deposed little dictator
who will be beheaded by the horizon.

At once my soul is opaque and leaden
and hollow and heathen.
The stabbing pain of the setting sun
forces my eyes shut
and being in the middle of a traffic jam,
I just close my eyes.
But even with sealed eyelids
I see the afterimage of the sun
which then splits into two, three, and then seven suns.
During this ride home
there are no exits,
no alternative routes, no trains, it's just this or nothing.
This eternal tollway is the only way home.